MAJOR ISSUES
AND
THE FACTS

by

Robert Gossman

authorHOUSE®

AuthorHouse™
1663 Liberty Drive, Suite 200
Bloomington, IN 47403
www.authorhouse.com
Phone: 1-800-839-8640

First published by AuthorHouse 7/28/2008

ISBN: 978-1-4389-0583-9 (sc)

Library of Congress Control Number: 2008907175
Printed in the United States of America
Bloomington, Indiana

This book is printed on acid-free paper.

Contents

THE ROLE OF GOVERNMENT

Preface

America is faced with multiple international and domestic challenges having major short term and long term impact on our country and its citizens. Because of the United States' leadership role among nations, these are also important elsewhere.

The focus of this book is on political and economic issues. Most of these matters are complex and often misunderstood. Furthermore, they are seldom analyzed and presented without bias. The purpose of this book is to inform the reader regarding these issues as clearly as possible and as comprehensively as is practical.

The facts are based on government data, library research, newspaper accounts, and a variety of public sources. Interpretation of the material is the work of the author.

The author has a degree in political science and years of executive business experience. A portion of the royalty proceeds from this book will be donated to charity.

To tell the truth.....

MAJOR ISSUES

and

THE FACTS

THE U.S. ECONOMY

Statistics are meaningful and valuable but must be viewed in perspective. People tend to extract specific numbers to make a point, and although the statistic is correct it is not the whole story. Politicians are noted for using this technique to advance their argument.

It is true that only five percent unemployment represents seven million workers who want a job but do not have one at the time. But in perspective **95%** or more than 140 million of the willing and able do have a job. From a non-statistical view the majority of those employed feel the economy is doing okay (though it could be better) while the unemployed person feels like he or she is in an economic recession, at least temporarily.

While perfection is a worthy goal, it is seldom achievable. This axiom applies to our national economy, which is the greatest in the history of the world. The U.S. economy is expansive and diverse. It also is made up of segments that may be up or down at different times. Some portions of the economy are very dynamic, changing drastically and fairly quickly, while others are stable.

The economy goes through cycles but they are irregular in occurrence and not predictable enough to avoid completely; however preventative and corrective actions can modify them. Down cycles are usually preceded by excesses.

We have the good fortune to live in a country with individual rights as opposed to state-owned resources and government control. Ours is a free market, private capital-based economy with free enterprise and virtually unlimited opportunity.

There are some very wealthy and some poor members of the population, but America differs from many other nations in having a very large middle class with a relatively high standard of living. Even the poor fare better than those in less developed countries.

Rhetoric by politicians and activists should be listened to with some skepticism. Most are motivated to push for change in government and usually for redistribution of wealth.

Our system is envied with its property rights, justice, capital and credit, open competition, employment and security for the citizens.

It is interesting that two thirds of the economy as measured by GDP is made up of consumer spending for products and services.

Personal income data are a bit misleading because of unreported income, part time employment, and the fact that individuals change jobs and move up the ladder then are replaced by others.

The personal savings rate of Americans is understated because it does not include vested pensions and home equity.

America can boast of a high home ownership rate with two thirds of households owning their residence. Interest rates for mortgages have been relatively low for years. Currently, there is a credit crunch brought on by lending excesses but even now well over 90% of mortgages are still paid on time.

There are 150 million registered personal vehicles in America. Demand for mobility and providing the related transportation infrastructure in the U.S. is unmatched.

Our population has grown to 300 million people. The ten most populated states in order are: California, Texas, New York, Florida, Illinois, Pennsylvania, Ohio, Michigan, Georgia, and North Carolina.

Employment in the category called "service sector" (as separate from manufacturing and agriculture) has grown to 80 percent of total employment. U.S.

unemployment is below that of the European industrial nations.

U.S. Employment

Year	2000	2001	2002	2003	2004	2005	2006
Employed (in millions)	137	137	136	138	139	142	144
Employment rate (%)	96	95	94	94	95	95	95

Productivity as measured by dollar value of all goods and services (GDP) and the number of persons engaged in the production, continues to be favorable as capital investment and efficiency improve results.

Gross Domestic Product (GDP)

GDP is the market value of all products and services produced annually by a country.

Comparison of major countries GDP in 2007:

($ trillion)

United States	14.0
China	10.5
India	4.4
Japan	4.3
Germany	2.7
France	2.0
United Kingdom	2.0
Russia	1.9
Brazil	1.8
South Korea	1.2
Canada	1.2
Mexico	1.2

As for income distribution, 90% of individual tax returns report annual income below $100,000 while ten percent report higher incomes. Proportionate income taxes are discussed elsewhere in this book, but the wealthy do pay most of the taxes.

Among other factors, the U.S. economy is based on the free exchange of capital, which is becoming more international in scope. Foreign investors and countries choose to invest in American enterprises, properties, and debt securities including those of the federal government.

Corporations and Profit

America's largest public corporations include WalMart, Exxon Mobil, General Motors, General Electric, Citigroup and other leading international businesses. These five examples combined generate over one trillion dollars in annual revenue. They typically earn seven percent of sales in profit after tax. The profit is applied to shareholder dividends and reinvested in the business.

There are over twenty million small businesses in the U.S. These range from sole proprietors to sizable enterprises depending on various definitions of "small". Regardless, they are the source of most new jobs.

The costs of a business may be comprised of materials, labor, space, equipment, supplies, taxes, interest on debt, utilities, insurance, employee benefits, selling expense, accounting, engineering and product development.

Risk Capital

The stock market rises and declines. In the long term investment risk has been rewarded. The variations of the market are dependent on corporate earnings, interest rates, economic forecasts, availability of funds, employment levels, fundamental soundness of the enterprises, investor sentiment, and the effect of unforeseen events.

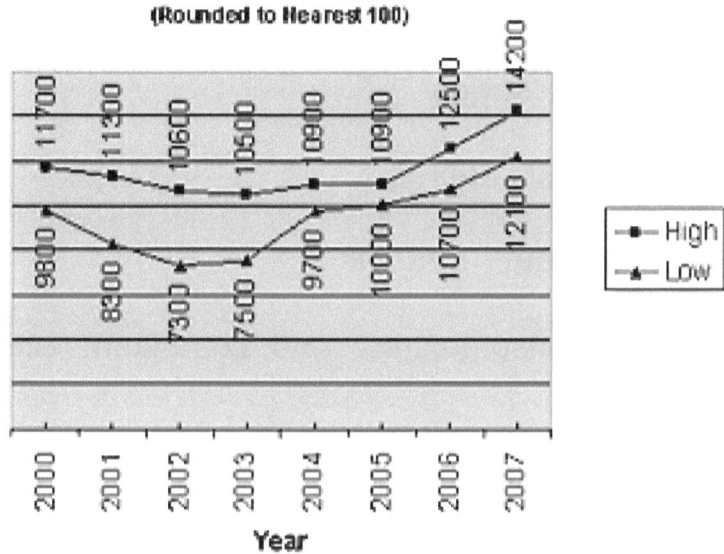

Dow Jones Industrial Average

(Rounded to Nearest 100)

The Commerce Department **Index of Leading Indicators** is evaluated by economists to look for economic change in future months. The leading indicators include measurement of the following:

Manufacturing labor hours

Unemployment claims

New orders for consumer and capital goods

Vendor delivery time

Building permits

Stock market prices

Money supply

Interest rates

Consumer outlook

There are also lagging and coincident economic indicators.

We have a high consumption society. U.S. personal consumption expenditures totaled nearly ten trillion dollars in 2007.

Recessions

An economic recession is defined as two consecutive calendar quarters or more with negative GDP (gross domestic product) growth. This situation has always involved higher unemployment. The official declaration of a recession does not happen until after it has occurred. An economic <u>depression</u> is much more severe and rare.

Recessions usually are several years apart and may last for less or more than a year. These economic cycles vary in depth and duration. They are brought on by a variety of conditions. Government cannot avoid recessions occurring but can mitigate its effect.

There was no recession in the recent five year period. The latest recessions were in 1990 and 2001 and had limited long term impact.

The current economic slowdown and credit squeeze in the housing industry is attributed to mortgage financing excesses, particularly sub-prime loans. Housing construction starts which have been as

high as two million units per year have fallen to an annual rate of one million during this slump.

Tax rates set by Congress do have a correlation to growth in the economy. It is a fact that lower income tax rates (under both Republican and Democratic administrations and Congresses) resulted in more revenue for the government as well as individual prosperity.

Job losses are caused by business failures from non-competitive labor costs, automation, lack of skills, excessive taxes and regulations, shortages of capital, and changes in market demand. In the past decade 15 million jobs were "lost" per year but 17 million new jobs were created per year, a net gain of millions.

Midwestern states with high taxes and restrictive union requirements have seen jobs move to more favorable southern states as well as beyond our borders.

Inflation

Inflation exists when prices are abnormally high and the purchasing power of the dollar is low. The **FRB** Federal Reserve central bank strives to temper inflation, control money supply and contribute to economic stability while encouraging moderate growth. It does this through setting interest rates and lending to banking institutions. The economy may be either in decline or growing in an inflationary period. Inflation and lower value of the dollar affect international and domestic trade.

The "core" rate of inflation excludes food and energy because those elements change drastically, but it's not as comprehensive as the CPI.

The **CPI** (consumer price index) measures the annual rate of price change for a combination of goods and services. In inflationary periods the prices of some commodities are higher while some may be lower, but the net effect is a broad increase in prices.

Consumer Price Index	Change
(Year)	(+%)
2003	2.3
2004	2.7
2005	3.4
2006	3.2
2007	4.1

Poverty

During the past five years about 35 million people in the U.S. lived below the income standard for poverty at any one time. This represents 12.5 percent of the population. Non-whites and under-educated persons are disproportionately high in numbers.

Poverty, lower education levels, and households without a complete family structure are linked to the higher crime rates found in declining neighbor-hoods.

In 2008 the income standard for poverty is $10,400 for one person and $17,600 for a family of three. The federal minimum wage is $6.55 per hour.

Trade

In America's history, restricting trade through tariffs rather than pursuing fair trade agreements has proven to have very adverse effect. The infamous Smoot-Hawley tariffs in the 1930's worsened the Great Depression and increased U.S. unemployment. There always will be countries which can produce certain goods at lower cost, because of their natural resources and cheaper labor.

The Kennedy Round of Tariffs negotiated in 1964 reduced trade duties or tariffs in 60 countries to great benefit.

NAFTA, the North American Free Trade Agreement, is the latest example of positive accomplishment. Since 1993, trade with Canada and Mexico has increased substantially. An additional benefit of NAFTA is we have first rights to buy oil from Canada and Mexico.

North American trade has contributed in part to an increase of millions of new U.S. jobs in that time period. Efforts to blame job losses on NAFTA are ignoring other reasons that manufacturing has lost jobs in an area due to high taxes, union demands and other factors. As a matter of fact, more than half of some states' exports go to Canada and Mexico.

Overall, 42% of U.S. exports go to countries where we have beneficial free trade agreements, while those countries generate less than ten percent of the world's GDP.

Our exports amount to one trillion dollars per year and imports total almost two trillion. Major import items are oil, vehicles, office equipment and televisions. The value of the dollar versus other currencies affects the amount of exports and imports, depending upon whether the comparative currency value is high or low.

A political argument is made that we do not put enough pressure on certain other countries in our trade agreements on issues such as pollution and human rights.

THE FEDERAL BUDGET

2006 Expenditures

The President and Office of Management and Budget (OMB) submit a proposed budget for all departments to Congress which modifies it, approves it and subsequently appropriates the funds.

The Congressional Budget Office issues long term projections of surplus or deficit, but these have proved to be inaccurate as conditions and assumptions change.

In the past five years federal spending has increased by **42%**.

2006 Federal Budget
($ Billions)
Total 2,655

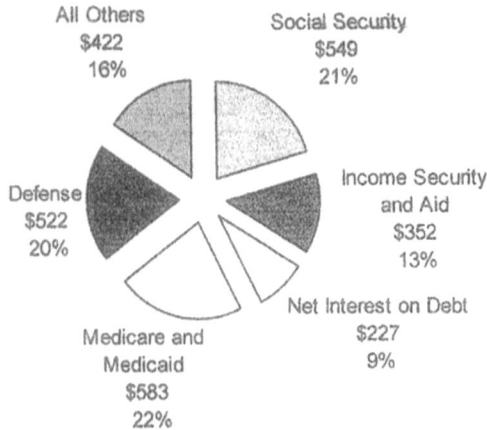

All Others
$422
16%

Social Security
$549
21%

Defense
$522
20%

Income Security
and Aid
$352
13%

Net Interest on Debt
$227
9%

Medicare and
Medicaid
$583
22%

($ Billions)

Revenues	2002	%	2006	%
Individual Income Taxes	$858	46	$1,044	43
Social Security	$701	38	$838	35
Corporate Income Taxes	$148	8	$354	15
Excise Taxes and Other	$147	8	$171	7
Total Receipts	**$1,853**	**100**	**$2,404**	**100**

($ Billions)

Expenditures	2002	%	2006	%
Social Security	$456	23	$549	21
Income Security and Aid	$313	16	$352	13
Medicare (2)	$231	11	$330	12
Medicaid	$197	10	$253	10
Defense (3)	$348	17	$522	20
Education (4)	$71	4	$119	4
Transportation Systems	$62	3	$70	3
Vetran Benefits	$51	3	$70	3
Disaster Relief	$4	0	$46	2
Net Interest on Debt	$171	9	$217	9
International, Science, Environment, Agriculture, Justice, and all other	$107	5	$120	5
Total Expenditures	**$2,011**	**100**	**$2,655**	**100**

Expenditures

(1) Includes individual and employer contributions.

(2) Includes prescription drug coverage.

(3) Includes the war in Iraq and Afghanistan.

(4) State and local government pay over 80% of the cost of public education.

(5) Net after interest income on treasury deposits.

Debt and Deficits

The U.S. public debt at the end of 2006 was $8.5 trillion which is equal to 65% of our annual GDP gross domestic product.

The budget deficit for the year was **$248** billion, representing **2%** of GDP or 9% of total government expenditures. A deficit increases debt; a surplus could be used to reduce debt.

Revenues from taxes and total spending each amount to about 20% of annual GDP.

It is necessary to borrow money to cover the amount of deficits. There is a growing trend among foreign governments as well as foreign investors to buy U.S. government debt bonds, and invest in American based businesses when permitted to do so. For example, sovereign wealth funds (from the boom in China and Middle East oil revenues) hold billions of dollars in U. S. bonds and corporate equity. The value of the dollar is adversely affected by excessive U.S. borrowing.

United Nations Contribution

The U.S. share of the U.N. budget is about 25%, second largest to Japan's contribution. Five billion dollars of the U.N. budget goes for peacekeeping which is criticized as to its effectiveness. Five billion dollars is for staff and administration which has grown significantly.

The U.N. consists of 192 different countries, and does administer some essential worldwide aid programs.

There have been scandals and questionable financial dealings by U.N. officials.

TAXES

The source of funds for government is taxes plus any borrowing. In 2006 the following taxes were paid in:

	$ billions	% of total
Individual Income Taxes	1,044	43
Social Security	838	35
Corporate Income Taxes	354	15
Excise Taxes and Other	171	7
Total Revenue	**2,407**	**100**

Current federal personal income tax rates range from zero to 35%. Corporate tax rates range from

15% to 35% on net income, among the highest in the world. State and local income taxes vary within states from 0% to 9.5%. States also may have sales and property taxes.

Listening to critics you would think the U.S. does not have a progressive rate tax system, but the wealthy do pay proportionately higher taxes than the less fortunate, and the poor pay little or none as it should be.

It is also true that cutting taxes results in economic growth and more government revenue. Simultaneously, more jobs are created.

Rich versus Poor

American people are generous in their charitable contributions, and the federal budget shows billions of government dollars in aid to the needy.

The latest data on the source of federal income tax revenues paid in by income level is for 2006.

Level of Taxpayers' Income	Share of Income	**Share of Taxes Paid**
Top 1%	21%	**39%**
Top 5%	36%	**60%**

The Top 40% of income recipients pay over 90% of taxes paid.

The bottom wage earners pay 1% of all income tax.

Those earning $20,000 to $200,000 pay 47% of the taxes.

There is general dissatisfaction with the increasing disparity of executive pay levels exceeding a standard of reasonableness.

Total revenues grew in the years following tax rate cuts due to growth being stimulated.

Effects of Tax Cuts

Tax cuts in the Kennedy, Reagan, and Bush administrations approved by Congress produced growth in the GDP, employment and federal revenue receipts for extended periods of time.

The latest 2003 income tax reduction legislation resulted in **17% to 20%** tax reductions for individuals earning $40,000 or less annually. Higher earning taxpayers received an average **11%**

reduction.

The long standing tax deduction for mortgage interest encourages home ownership.

Capital gains tax cuts to 15% for long term gains (over one year) yielded a dramatic increase in such federal revenues from the increased investments made. Note that two thirds of American adults now own shares of capital stocks directly or in retirement accounts. Recently 80% of the tax returns that included capital gains had household incomes under $100,000. As the stock market rose to record levels, previous capital gains tax cuts by other administrations also stimulated the economy and increased tax revenue.

Unfortunately, as revenues grew so did federal spending which resulted in deficits, but it is argued the deficits are not excessive as a percentage of GDP or the total economy. The deficits could have been avoided or reduced by lower growth in spending.

The cost of the Iraq Wars contributed to the spending increases. Including budgets for previously neglected military needs, defense spending increased from 2002 to 2006 from 17% to a 20% share of the total budget.

Current System Faults

The Alternative Minimum Tax (AMT) was enacted thirty nine years ago to adjust for only a few high income taxpayers who avoided paying any tax after allowed deductions. With no provision for future inflation effect, this tax now would apply to **twenty** million households if not exempted by Congress. This law has higher rates and very limited deductions for those earning $75,000 or more per year.

In addition, there exists an estate tax which applies to large and relatively small inheritances whose assets were previously subjected to income tax, thus a form of double taxation.

Year 2010

The 2003 tax cuts legislation will expire in 2010 if not extended or made permanent. This tax increase on wealthy and middle income taxpayers would yield a reduction in any future deficits (if not spent) but also would affect economic expansion, employment and thus revenues. More effective would be a reduction in just the rate of growth in government spending.

Complexity

The U.S. tax code contains more than 5,000 pages. Untold man hours and expense are involved in accounting, analyzing, and preparing tax returns. The IRS is a large bureaucracy required to administer the tax code. In comparison, Canada has 2,400 pages of tax code, Germany 1,700, and France 1,300. Enforcement is another problem, and auditing is selective.

Changing the regulations is difficult, but an overhaul and simplification are clearly needed.

SOCIAL SECURITY AND HEALTHCARE

Social Security

Social Security was enacted in 1935 toward the end of the Great Depression, a time in which many people had no job. Contrary to some misinterpretations it was not intended to provide full retirement income for workers, the plan was to cover a portion of retirement income security for the bulk of the older adult population. Revenue would come from a tax on both employers and employees.

The biggest problem with Social Security today is that the number of retirees will continue increasing, particularly with the "baby boomers" born after World War II, and the number of workers paying into the fund will not sustain the benefits increase.

Furthermore, the past surplus in Social Security revenues has been borrowed by the Federal government to help offset spending deficits in the U.S. budget.

Medicare has been added to the Social Security program and its costs are growing every year. Making changes in the present plan is very difficult politically, especially in the prevailing partisan environment with Congress and the administration.

Other contributing factors to the problem include the fact we are living longer, and our great economy produces more with less labor required thus fewer contributors.

Social Security benefits now average $2,000 monthly per recipient and the number qualified as recipients exceeds 41 million people. This does not include over seven million who are on welfare and not eligible for Social Security.

The standard retirement age (if not disabled) is now 67 years, or less if born before 1938 (under the original plan) thus eligible for earlier retirement at 62 to 65 from the prior schedule.

More fortunate retirees have some combination of Social Security and pension or savings. Government tax deferral policy encourages IRA individual retirement accounts and 401K

supplemental retirement programs that may be contributed to by the employer and employee. Others add to their retirement income with part time employment or investment income.

Social security tax revenue totals over $600 billion per year and disbursements in 2006 were $450 billion, but the expenditure rate is growing more rapidly than the funding. Projections indicate a deficit by the year 2017. Corrections to avoid a crisis should be planned well ahead to minimize the effect on individuals now and later.

Other federal welfare or aid programs include veteran benefits, unemployment compensation, and food stamps for the poor.

The tax rate for both Social Security and Medicare has been raised over time to its present level of 7.65 percent of earnings by the employee plus 7.65 percent by the employer, a total of more than fifteen percent. This applies to the first $97,500 of earnings in 2007 and this level is scheduled to be increased.

The solution to the situation of lower revenue and higher Social Security expenditures involves all or part of the following potential adjustments:

Raise the retirement age to some degree.

Raise the income level that is taxable.

Means test and reduce benefits for those not in need.

Provide optional investment of a portion of individual accounts for a higher rate of return.

Reduce the growth rate of inflation adjust ments.

The alternatives are to raise taxes and/or reduce benefits.

Medicare

Medicare insures 43 million elderly and disabled citizens. With the increase in our elderly population and the growing number of retirees, plus the increasing cost of medical care and the added prescription drug benefit, federal revenues and disbursements indicate future growing deficits. In 2008 for the first time, revenue from taxes for Part A hospital care will not cover the current expenditures by the government so the present surplus will be tapped.

Medicare Part A pays for qualified hospital care and eligibility starts at age 65.

Part B covers other medical costs such as doctors and tests, but the person must pay for the option with a monthly premium.

Part C is an alternative benefit plan based on use of a "managed care" or HMO health maintenance organization.

Part D prescription drug coverage was introduced in 2006, with a monthly premium charge of about $22 plus the patient paying a portion of the costs of medication. The cost will be increased as necessary. Prices for the 200 most popular prescription drugs rose seven percent in 2006 and again in 2007, although generic prescriptions cost less.

Private supplemental insurance plans are available to cover some of the costs not included in Medicare.

When our system is compared to other countries with government-

run medicine, our patient care and medical developments produce better results with lower taxes but the total cost is relatively high. The challenge is for the U.S. system of private enterprise and government subsidies to reduce cost, without adversely affecting healthcare quality.

Medicaid

Over 35 million people who cannot afford healthcare and are not eligible for Medicare are covered by Medicaid. The federal government pays 57% of the expense while the states pay the remainder and administer the program.

Healthcare

America's privately based healthcare system is clearly among the best in the world. Nearly 90% of Americans with some form of government or private health insurance are satisfied with the quality of service they receive. Among other countries which have socialized medicine, the services are paid for with higher taxes and typically 75% of healthcare compensation is through government funds. The patients in those countries have numerous complaints.

Politicians and critical activists in the U.S. refer to **44** million **uninsured**. Many of these are non-citizens including illegal aliens, and even they get emergency care. Over 14 million of the uninsured live in households that earn more than $50,000 a year and could afford some insurance. Millions more are young adults who do not feel they need health insurance. An additional number fail to apply for Medicaid although they are eligible. Special programs are offered for children.

Some individuals are uninsured for a short period of time between job changes or other temporary gaps in coverage. The net result is less than **ten** million are without health insurance at any one time for reasons other than personal choice.

Cost

There is a serious problem with the rising cost of healthcare which far exceeds the rise in inflation. About $1 trillion is spent per year in public funds and over $1 trillion more by private funds. This is 16% of GDP. After the effect of baby boomer retiring and at the present rate of growth in medical costs, this two trillion dollars is forecast to double by 2017.

Part of the rise in costs is for new technology such as scanning devices and new drug development. Hospitals also have invested heavily in expansion, upgrades and new facilities. However, the greatest operating cost for hospitals is personnel.

The breakdown of all medical expenditures shows approximately 30% for hospital care, 20% for doctor fees, 10% for prescription medication; the 40% remaining includes dental, nursing homes, administrative expense, etc. Therapeutic drug usage has been growing (not related to illegitimate use).

Pricing of medical services is not under control, but is influenced by Medicare approval limits, insurance companies and regional completion. States restrict insurance companies through regulation.

Millions of employees and retirees are insured under employer sponsored benefit plans. These vary widely in benefits; some are through HMO's and PPO preferred provider programs, with some in new HSA health savings accounts. Sixty percent of companies offer health benefit plans.

In 2007 employers paid an average $9,000 annual insurance premium for a family's coverage and the employee paid $3,000. Due to rising costs, employers are raising the employee contribution amount.

Despite America's generally fine healthcare and longer survival rates, there is considerable room for improvement. By far the leading causes of death are heart disease and cancer, followed by strokes, respiratory diseases and accidents. Preventative medicine and avoidance of unhealthy habits reduces treatment cost and suffering.

IMMIGRATION

The new America was founded by immigrants. They always have been a source of growth and advancement in our society. Diversity is one of our strengths with a heritage made up mostly of European civilization. Our parentage is German, Irish, English, Italian, Polish and other. Recent influxes have been Asian and Hispanic.

The U.S. population today has nearly 40 million foreign born residents. The largest group (approximately one third) is from Mexico. An estimated **12** million Mexican immigrants are here illegally, willing to work for low wages and in less desirable jobs.

These illegal immigrants come here to work in construction, the hospitality industry, manufacturing ,agriculture, retail business, and service occupations. As many as half of them are in the border states of California, and Texas, plus Florida.

They do present a burden on those areas for schools, healthcare, etc.

Legal immigrants include many non-citizens who are in the U.S. for purposes of education or temporary work, as well as those who are seeking to become citizens. Congress limits their number.

The immigration laws passed long ago by Congress are not well enforced today. The number of illegals is overwhelming. There is general consensus that particularly the southern border must be closed for hundreds if not thousands of miles. There is little agreement about what to do with the millions of illegal immigrants who are already here.

Issues to be considered are how to identify them, how long they have been here, what is their contribution to our workforce, which ones should and can be deported, what requirements must be met for citizenship and what penalties should be assessed for their transgression of the law.

These problems are difficult to resolve, and more so in the partisan political environment existing in Washington.

THE MIDDLE EAST

Of the sixteen countries, the largest in land area are the Kingdom of Saudi Arabia, the Islamic Republic of Iran, the Arab Republic of Egypt, and the Republic of Turkey.

The most populated country in the Middle East at 80 million is Egypt. Most of the populations in all the countries live in urban areas. Some of the countries have a high percentage of residents who were not born there.

With partial exceptions and notably in all of Iran where the predominant religion is Shiite Muslim, the majority in the Middle East are Sunni Muslim. Overall, more than 90% in the Middle East adhere to the Islam religion.

The principal languages (in order) are Arabic, Turkish, Persian (Farsi), and Kurdish. The ethnic makeup of the area is about 50% Arabs, 20% Turks, the remainder are mixed origins.

Middle East

As you know,

Saudi Arabia is the greatest oil producer.

Turkey has the largest military.

The history of Egypt dates back beyond 4000 B.C.

Iranians are considered Persian, not Arab.

Kurds consider themselves ethnically independent.

Israeli-Palestinian Conflict

In 1948 at the end of World War II, the state of Israel was recognized internationally and the British mandate over Palestine ended.

Israel was attacked by Arab forces from Egypt, Syria, Jordan, Saudi Arabia, Lebanon, and Iraq. The attackers were defeated in a short time. Egypt and Syria attacked Israel again in 1973 unsuccessfully. Hundreds of thousands of Palestinians were uprooted; many of Jordan's citizens are Palestinians.

The **Occupied Territories** now controlled by Israel (but with a Palestinian population) are in the widely separated coastal Gaza Strip and the West Bank of the Jordan River. Included in the West Bank is Jerusalem, a holy city for Christians, Jews, and Muslims.

In peace negotiations, the Palestinian authority has rejected Israeli offers of land and opportunity to establish a Palestinian state in exchange for peace. The militant groups Fatah and Hamas in the occupied territories, Hezbollah in Syria and Lebanon, and the Iranian Islamic regime have publicly vowed to annihilate Israel.

The Nazi Germany holocaust "exterminated" six million European Jews in World War II. There are now approximately five million Jews in Israel, and five million in the United States.

The U.S. has exercised restraint in trying to achieve peace through diplomacy, but it is time for the Arab League to push for a settlement of the issue. Our policy is to support Israel as it has been established after World War II, and encourages establishment of a peaceful Palestinian state.

ISLAM

History

The prophet **Muhammad** lived in Mecca around 600 A.D., was married and became an Arabian political leader. He was "called by Allah" to minister and teach religion. Muhammad and his believers regarded Abraham, Moses and Jesus as earlier prophets.

After his death, Muslim armies spread the faith into other countries in the 600's and 700's.

Tenets of Islam

Islam requires total surrender to the one

God Allah for inner peace.

The Koran (Quran) is the holy book of Islam.

Followers seek social justice.

Sharia holy law supersedes sectarian laws.

In a Jihad or holy war, martyrs go to heaven.

Muhammad preached tolerance for other faiths.

Women and marriage are protected.

Five Pillars of Islam

There is but one God.

Faithful must pray five times each day.

Charity: 2 ½ % or 1/40th of one's wealth is to be given to the poor.

Observe the Ramadan holy month.

Pilgrimage to Mecca once in life is required if able.

Prevalence

Among the world's population of 7 billion, over 1.3 billion are of the Muslim religion. For comparison, over 2.2 billion are Christian, half of which are Catholic, 1 billion non-declared for any faith, 900 million Hindu, and the remainder connected with other religions.

The Republic of Indonesia population of 235 million is 87% Muslim, the most populated Muslim country, surpassing Egypt.

Factions

After Muhammad's death, the majority Arabian **Sunnis** recognized succeeding "caliphs" as rulers. The minority **Shiites** chose Ali, Muhammad's cousin and son-in-law as leader. Ali's son was killed in a battle between the two factions and is a source of conflict yet today, centuries later.

Iran and Iraq are populated by mostly Shia, while all other Muslim country populations are majority Sunni.

Through the Wahabbi movement based in Arabia, Islam is taught in the school systems and religious practices permeate Arab life.

Political Factors

Islam appears vulnerable to the use or misuse of religion as a rationale for achieving political goals.

Lack of separation of state and religion leads to problems of excessive power, and the fervency of believers is difficult to restrain. It is claimed injustices are caused by lack of religious dedication, and there is a sense of humiliation in the Arab culture for any failures.

Islam has been growing worldwide as a religion but attempts to impose Islam through government have failed in countries where open elections are held.

TERRORISM

Definition

Terrorism is instilling fear with ruthless, shocking acts of violence against innocent victims in committing crime or in war. The dictionary says "the use of force or threats to demoralize, intimidate, coerce by filling the subjects with terror". Such murder and mayhem are prohibited in civilized countries by laws and moral codes of conduct.

There is no one cause or motivation for terrorism. It may come from political belief, to achieve power, or for revenge, greed, envy, personal ambition, to redress a grievance, win a rivalry, display hate, or misguided advocacy of religion. Some individuals use it just to demonstrate their strength and brutality, others may be seeking retribution for perceived ill treatment, real or imagined.

Examples of terrorism are the bombing of vehicles, launching of rockets indiscriminately into civilian areas, beheadings on video, suicide bombers in marketplaces, kidnapping for political purpose, anthrax in mail, and gang shootings. Our subject matter is political and religious terrorism, not individual crime.

The current weapon of choice for terrorists is explosive devices, which require limited technical knowledge, are available or can be created readily and cause extensive damage. Terrorists do not subscribe to rules of war such as the Geneva Convention agreed to by most civilized countries.

Terrorism is used widely by **radical** fundamentalist Islamists to achieve political goals in the name of religion. They cite other historic movements such as the Crusades and admit Islam was sometimes spread "by the sword." However, **jihad** or holy war is invoked to destroy non-believers if they do not convert and submit. Actually, Muhammad and the Koran teach not to attack, but to make war only in self-defense. There are also express rules in the Koran against mutilation and for sparing the innocent.

We are learning that strategies of deterrence and containment don't work with amorphous, loosely linked and dispersed networks of cells of radicals.

Recent Terrorist Acts

As far back as 1979 Iranian radicals seized the American embassy in Tehran and held hostages. At that time Islamic terrorists also seized the Grand Mosque in Mecca, Saudi Arabia, until government forces retook it with many killed.

In 1983 Hezbollah "Army of God" suicide truck bombings were used in Lebanon resulting in 300 dead.

During the 1980's a TWA airliner was hijacked by Hezbollah; other air flights and airports were attacked by Pakistan militants. Over 400 people were killed by Libyans, in the Pan Am explosion over Lockerbie and in a French flight from Africa.

The first World Trade Center bombing occurred in 1993 by Sunni extremist followers of the blind sheik Abdel-Rahman.

In 1998 two U.S. embassies in East Africa were bombed by Al Qaeda.

It should be noted the Oklahoma federal building truck bombing by McVeigh and Nichols was the work of Americans.

9/11/2001

On this date the Al Qaeda terrorists hijacked four jetliners, destroyed the World Trade Center, damaged the Pentagon (and one plane was downed by passenger resistance). This attack on U.S. soil by Al Qaeda murdered 3,000 people.

In the early 2000's an Indonesian resort was bombed by Islamists, Chechen rebels attacked within Russia, Al Qaeda bombings were perpetrated in Saudi Arabia and Morocco, British offices in Turkey were bombed. Chechen rebels also attacked a school in Russia.

From 2004 to 2006 Al Qaeda bombed trains in Madrid, buses in London, and hotels in Jordan. Trains were also bombed in Mumbai, India by the "Army of Terror".

For multiple years rockets were launched into Israel by Hezbollah from Lebanon, and suicide bombers by Hamas entered Israel from the Gaza Strip.

Some terrorists come from the Muslim Brotherhood in Egypt.

Al Qaeda

Al Qaeda is an international radical Islamist organization, overtly on the offensive against the United States and Israel in particular. Long before 9/11/01 they attacked our embassies in Kenya and Tanzania (in 1998). In 2000, they attacked the USS Cole in Yemen. Al Qaeda declared war against the U.S. in 1999 for its support of Israel and presence in Saudi Arabia. But they use unconventional warfare without uniforms or standing armies, no code of conduct, disregard for territories, and employing non-traditional weapons.

The leader of Al Qaeda is Osama Bin Laden, a son of a prosperous family and construction enterprise in Saudi Arabia. Osama fought the Russians in Afghanistan. By 1994 Osama was a radical Islamist, outspoken against the western world, and exiled by the Saudis to Sudan. Osama began financing terrorism. In 1996 Sudan expelled him to Afghanistan. He later sought safe haven in Yemen. In Afghanistan he collaborated with the Taliban. Osama now is somewhere in the mountainous tribal region between Afghanistan and Pakistan. Opportunities to kill or capture him have failed or been missed. The number two "most wanted" leader of Al Qaeda is an Egyptian doctor, Al Zawahiri.

It has been estimated there are five thousand or so loosely affiliated members of the Al Qaeda network around the world. Prior to the U.S. invasion of Afghanistan in response to the 9/11 attacks, Al

Qaeda had a headquarters and training resources in that country. They now hope to establish an organized presence in Iraq by resisting the U.S. occupation and sectarian democracy there.

In addition to their attempt to take advantage of the instability in Iraq and Afghanistan, Al Qaeda is trying to foment trouble in Pakistan.

9/11 Commission Report

The independent bi-partisan report of this commission appointed by the President and Congress contains about 600 pages of detailed information. It concludes there was and is a real threat toward us and our values by Islamic terrorism. It goes further in identifying failures in our intelligence system and lack of action by the government, and makes recommendations.

Bin Laden and Zawahiri issued a declaration of war against America in 1998. At that time Al Qaeda was building an organization structure from Afghanistan. Rumors were circulating that Al Qaeda was planning aircraft hijackings. For international political reasons, U.S. military action was discouraged. In early 2001 there were numerous classified reports of aggressive plans being developed by Bin Laden's followers in various countries.

The 19 hijackers of 9/11 were relatively young Muslims, most of Saudi origin, who were promised heavenly rewards for their action. They were modestly financed, led by an Al Qaeda cell planner, and a leader of implementation. Four obtained flight training in the U.S. and others had training in other countries. Their weapons were common box cutter knives, their tactic was pretending to be normal visitors.

As for intelligence, the U.S. relied heavily on foreign sources. Domestic FBI information was required to be kept separate from the CIA and other U.S. agencies based on a legal opinion within the Justice Department.

After the 9/11 attack the U.S. administration and military attacked Al Qaeda in Afghanistan, calling it the first step in a war on terrorism.

Following the commission report, the U.S. has been implementing most of their recommendations regarding intelligence, diplomacy, policy position against radical Islam expansion, and strengthening homeland security.

U.S. Counter-Terrorism Plan

Our government has a plan for combating terror, much of which is not classified secret. It recognizes there will be military conflicts plus a battle of ideas.

The strategies are to support democracies, prevent attacks by terrorist networks; deny terrorists control, support and sanctuary in rogue states; and ensure weapons of mass destruction are not available to terrorists.

We have made progress in degrading the effectiveness of Al Qaeda, but the terrorist threat is broader than one network. The terrorist movement at large is fueled by a desire to replace American world leadership with Muslim rule. Radical Islamists use distorted religious beliefs to justify violence, hate, and aggression.

The U.S. has liberated 50 million Afghanis and Iraqis, although the battle is not over to establish tranquility there. We are enlisting partners in the political, economical and military effort to deal with international terrorism. We still have 30,000 troops in Afghanistan and at present 160,000 in Iraq with some scheduled to start withdrawing as conditions permit.

Internally, we are consolidating homeland security, integrating and improving intelligence. Action has been taken in our airports, the southern border is being addressed, but port cargo security is still lacking.

The FISA Foreign Intelligence Surveillance Act permits our NSA National Security Agency to monitor international messages, and the FISA Court can issue special search warrants against suspected terrorists. Members of Congress have been briefed on authorized interrogation techniques.

IRAQ

Background

Iraq is surrounded by six different countries of the Middle East. It suffered ancient conquests by Russians, Greeks, Arabs, Mongols and Turks.

Iraq's recent history starts with Saddam Hussein's dictatorship, and oppression by the Sunni secular Baath party for more than two decades. This began in 1979, the same year as the Islamic revolution in Iran.

In 1981, Israeli aircraft bombed a nuclear reactor facility in Iraq, putting it out of commission.

A war between Iran and Iraq lasting from 1980 to 1988 resulted in deaths of hundreds of thousands.

In August 1990, the Iraq army attacked Kuwait claiming it as Iraq territory. The U.S. with UN support liberated Kuwait in February 1991. This has been referred to as the Persian Gulf War.

During the 1990's the UN conducted intermittent nuclear inspections, and multiple UN resolutions condemning Iraq weapons programs met with little success.

U.S. and British military aircraft enforced a no-fly zone over Iraq under a UN decree.

Subsequent Action

The U.S. and a coalition of other nations invaded Iraq in 2003 and dismantled the army. Despite intelligence to the contrary, weapons of mass destruction were not found, but the Iraqi people were freed. Other rationale for the invasion is discussed later in this chapter.

Sovereignty was handed over to the new Iraqi government in 2004. Elections were held and a constitution established in 2005.

Meanwhile resentful Sunnis and vengeful Shia created violent conflict, as the U.S. and its allies attempted to establish order and begin reconstruction. In 2006 the important Shiite Golden Mosque shrine was bombed by the minority Sunnis, and cleric Al Sadr's Shiite militia engaged in anti-American fighting.

Today there are 160,000 U.S. troops in Iraq and violence has declined, but U.S. public support of such a prolonged conflict has turned negative, and political progress by the Iraqis is slow. The total size of the U.S. military is approximately the same as it was in the year 2000.

The new Iraqi military count is up to 200,000 with a plan to double in number as training progresses. This does not include the police force.

By comparison, the number of Americans serving in World War II, Korea and Vietnam was in the millions and deaths in the tens of thousands. But the Gulf Wars have been very costly in dollars, and 4,000 American lives have been lost. The cost of this five year protracted engagement is approaching a trillion dollars.

The loss of Iraqi lives including civilians has been grossly exaggerated in some reports. The World Health Organization has estimated about 150,000 deaths but the Iraq Body Count group

estimates 50,000. There have also been over one million Iraqi refugees who fled to Jordan, Syria and other adjacent countries.

Some of the post-invasion problems in Iraq were foreseen. In 2002 the U.S. administration did do an evaluation of possible adverse consequences of attacking Iraq. Things considered included (1) that WMD weapons of mass destruction might not be found, (2) stabilization and reconstruction could take years, and (3) Iran and Syria could help our enemies. The new U.S. policy of preemptive attack may be disputed, and the decision to launch the offensive may not have been wise, but various unpredictable results had been contemplated.

The likely consequence of **premature U. S. withdrawal** now would be destabilization, and a multi-nation war between Sunni and Shia Muslims could ensue. Major sources of oil would become involved, and the conflict would expand in the whole region.

The Iraq Study Group Report

A group of distinguished and experienced leaders from various U.S. roles issued an analysis and recommendations for the situation in Iraq as of 2006, which are pertinent yet in 2008.

The **violence** was and is fed by Sunni versus Shia sectarian conflict, Al Qaeda penetration, widespread criminality, plus interference by Iran and Syria. Progress toward self-government and pacification by the newly elected Iraqi government was and is painfully slow.

The **consequences of failure** to bring the situation to a successful conclusion and ultimate withdrawal of U.S. forces include: an increase in adverse intervention by neighboring countries, even more sectarian violence, gains by Al Qaeda terrorists, continued instability in the Middle East, and loss of standing in the world for America.

The Iraqi army and police must achieve more control, the Al Sadr Shiite militia needs to be subdued; and the Iraqi government accomplish more reconciliation among the majority Shia, minority Sunni and Kurdish factions.

Saudi Arabia and the other Persian Gulf states should contribute more to reconstruction in Iraq, and more Iraq oil revenues should go to rebuilding infrastructure.

Since Saddam Hussein was removed, Iraq has held elections for representative government, established a constitution, and is dividing oil revenues. More needs to be done.

In its 100 or so pages, the study group put forth 79 recommendations ranging from increased international diplomatic efforts such as those with Israel and Palestine, to specific milestones for improvement by the Iraq government in internal reconciliation, to reducing the role of the U.S. military.

Leadup to U.S. Invasion

The Middle East has long been a powder keg on the verge of explosion. The control of oil, mixture of religion and politics, lack of democracy, anti-Israel sentiment, Sunni-Shia rivalry, all contribute to the instability.

U.S. policy prior to the 9/11/2001 attack on our country by the radical Muslim terrorists was one of containment, and playing a leading role in the United Nations peace efforts. The U.S. led coalition that expelled Iraq after its invasion of Kuwait immediately withdrew after accomplishing the U.N. mandate in that regard.

Afghanistan

In the view of most, the U.S. attack on Al Qaeda's home base in Afghanistan was clearly justified. The greatest complication came from the need to oust the Taliban from power and support the establishment of a democracy. Though still difficult, this has been largely successful. In addition to the lingering fight with rebels, a fundamental problem exists with the economy's dependence on opium poppy revenue.

Regional Situation

Iran supports the Shiites in Iraq and wants to increase its influence. Iran has also supported terrorists, providing weapons plus explosive devices and training to militants as well as financial aid. Iran makes public threats against the U.S. and Israel, and is proceeding with nuclear development against UN resolutions.

Syria meddles in Lebanon affairs, supports Hezbollah and allows contraband material flows into Iraq.

The **Palestinians** and Hamas party have rejected Israel's offer of land for a Palestinian nation in return for guarantees of peace for Israel. They refuse to recognize Israel's right to exist.

Pakistan and **India** border confrontation has existed for years. Both are nuclear powers and allies of the U.S.

Saudi Arabia with its large share of oil reserves is run by a monarchy which strives to avoid conflict. The historic origin of Muhammad and Islam in Arabia make this Sunni country most important.

Egypt has the largest population of the Arab countries and is concerned about potential wars.

Jordan has the biggest Palestinian population but the government has been cooperative with the U.S. in its peace efforts.

Other Events

Saddam Hussein ruled Iraq as a despot, torturing and killing dissidents. He ordered the use of poison gas on Iraqi Kurds in the northern province. The Baath party government was secular and not radically religious.

In the 1980's Iraq instigated war with Iran. In the 1990's Iraq invaded Kuwait. In the same era, Hussein denied the U.N. weapons inspectors access. There were minor contacts between Iraq and Al Qaeda but little consequence.

In 1998 President Clinton ordered limited air strikes against Iraq weapons facilities.

Valerie Plame Incident

A mountain was made out of a molehill when a news story evolved into U.S. prosecution, over information about alleged attempts of Iraq to obtain raw uranium from Africa. The issue became whether Plame was a CIA secret agent, her husband Joe Wilson's fact finding mission, and who leaked her name to the press. It was all an overblown case of anti-war and political debate, with one conviction for misleading testimony after lengthy investigation.

Rationale for War

There are a number of myths about the reasons for the U.S. invasion of Iraq in 2003. Among these are that we wanted to take over a source of oil, that President Bush's advisors wanted to engage in another war, that the administration lied about our intelligence reports, and that the only cause for action was Iraq WMD weapons of mass destruction.

Time has proven our intention was not to possess the oil fields in Iraq. No proof has been found that the advisors or administration wanted war for political gain.

Intelligence

It is true that WMD were not found after some had been destroyed by U.N. weapons inspectors previously. However, the 2004 **Senate Intelligence Committee** report identified numerous failures of intelligence gathering and analysis. The 2005 Robb-Silverman report on WMD intelligence in particular came to the same conclusion. These bi-partisan investigations further found no evidence of administration pressure on the intelligence agencies to provide slanted information.

The NIE National Intelligence Estimates presented in 2002 stated Iraq continued its WMD programs in defiance of the U.N. and they had chemical and biological weapons as well as missiles, plus the potential for nuclear weapons in the near future. Intelligence from other countries agreed with such assessments. Saddam succeeded in fooling the whole world.

Reasons other than WMD

The Clinton and Bush presidencies both advocated promotion of democracy in Iraq and elsewhere.

Regime change to rid the country of brutality and oppression was one goal.

U.N. resolutions, multi-lateral diplomacy and economic sanctions had failed over a period of years. The effectiveness of the U.N. in world affairs was diminished by Iraq's arrogance. Secretary of State Colin Powell expressed the need for coalition military action in Iraq at the U.N. seeking support by the UN Security Council which was partially granted.

Middle East instability was worsened by Iraq's aggressions.

Democrat and Republican leaders in Congress publicly agreed Iraq was a threat to our national interests. Three fourths of our Senators voted for the joint resolution authorizing the use of force against Iraq.

History will determine whether the U.S. led war in Iraq was worthwhile, but the cause appeared to be worthy.

Post-Attack Developments

No one foresaw the prolonged nature of the war in Iraq and some of the turns of events. Mistakes were made after the initial battle success and are mentioned in the following section.

The trial and execution of Hussein and his henchmen was justly performed by the Iraqi court.

One interesting side effect of the invasion of Iraq was the complete change in direction of Libya, denouncing terrorism.

The National Strategy for Victory in Iraq published by the White House in 2003 defined the long term goal as a peaceful, united, stable and secure country, integrated into the international community and a partner in the war on terrorism. Interim goals were establishing democratic institutions, building a security force, meeting political milestones, reconstruction and economic growth.

The three tracks to victory are security, political and economic development. Success is a vital U.S. interest, failure is an unacceptable option. It will take time, and our military presence must be based on changing conditions.

Mistakes

The complete dismantling of old Iraq security forces could have been done differently, retaining some. Not confiscating weapons all over was a costly error, as was not disbanding Al Sadr's militia. The humiliating treatment (although not torture) by a handful of U.S. soldiers with poor supervision toward a few prisoners at Abu Ghraib was a major scandal and political embarrassment.

Progress

Infrastructure improvements have resulted in more electricity, water, sewers, and telephones being available to citizens. Oil production in the neglected and damaged oil fields has returned to pre-war levels, and oil revenues are being shared.

Casualties from the violence have declined dramatically in the past year. The government is taking action to suppress the insurgents.

Political reconciliation has been slow but is improving. Life for many in Baghdad and elsewhere is returning to normal, although unemployment is still high.

The foreign insurgents who came to Iraq during the postwar chaos are being defeated. Many Al Qaeda fighters have been killed there.

The U.S. military "surge" has involved the Iraqi military and security forces more. The purpose of the surge in forces was and is to stabilize by reducing violence and allowing more reconciliation politically. This redefined strategy under General Patreus is working. It includes increased cooperation with Iraqi citizens of all factions.

Everyone wants to see U.S. troops withdrawal beginning as soon as conditions on the ground in Iraq permit. In this American election year the debate is how fast it can be done. It is reasonable to ask for further clarification from the administration as to what criteria will permit significant troops withdrawals.

Consequences

Withdrawal too soon would encourage **Al Qaeda** who moved into Iraq. Bin Laden's former lieutenant Zarkawi (now deceased) tried to create a new front for their declared Islamist religious war against all infidels.

Local anti-American cleric **Al Sadr** could realize his political ambitions and conduct a civil war with his Shiite militia.

Iranian influence would dominate Iraq and give them more power in the region, with or without their nuclear threat.

Terrorism in the whole world would be strengthened because powerful America gave up and could not halt their ruthless methods. Life is not precious to fanatics.

Behind the scenes, the other Arab nations say they do not want Iran to possess nuclear weapons and they do not want the U.S. to withdraw from Iraq until it is stable. We need their support, but they need to contribute more.

IRAN

Iran is an important player in the Middle East saga, and wants to be even more influential.

It is the base of the Shia branch of the Muslim world, who are far outnumbered by the Sunni. Its government is really controlled by clerics and it is the source of much extremist Islam ideology.

Iran is sizable with a population of 65 million, over 600 thousand square miles of land, annual GDP of $600 billion (mostly from oil) and an army of more than 500 thousand. Originally Persian, the official language is Farsi.

History

Upon the death of the Shah in 1979 the sectarian government collapsed, and the exiled radical cleric Khomeini assumed power with an Islamic government. The seizure of the American embassy and holding of hostages was symbolic anti-Americanism.

During the 1980's an extensive war with neighboring Iraq resulted in hundreds of thousands of deaths.

The natural disaster of earthquakes in 1990 and 2003 killed tens of thousands of Iranians.

The Guardian Council in 2005 put Islamic fundamentalist Ahmadinejad in the figurehead presidency. He has threatened both Israel and the U.S. The current Ayotollah is named Khameini.

The United Nations approved sanctions to halt Iran's nuclear development, to no avail. Inspections by the IAEA International Atomic Energy Agency have been stymied.

Shiite Ambitions

While there is a fragmented struggle within the Muslim world between moderate and extremist Islamists, as well as between secular and theocratic structures of government, there is a centuries old conflict between Shia and the majority Sunni faction (although both advocate the spread of Islam).

Iraq has a large population of Shia, but Iran is the major Shia nation-state. Iranian leaders in the current time period have publicly declared goals of establishing a caliphate or religion based

government well beyond their present borders. Khameni and Ahmadinejad have expressed diatribes against Western culture, the United States, and Jews.

Iran has defied United Nations resolutions and International Atomic Energy Agency inspections regarding its nuclear development programs. The issue involves especially the operation of centrifuge facilities to enrich uranium to weapons grade. While this is not necessary for peaceful energy production, it would be necessary for the development of bombs and nuclear missiles.

U.S. policy is to stop the development of nuclear weapons using diplomatic pressure with other countries (and the U.N.), economic and financial sanctions, and reserves the right to use military force if provoked. The same policy (plus aid) has been applied to North Korea.

Iranian Power Plays

As a means of extending its influence, Iran promotes the instability in the Middle East. The fall of Saddham Hussein's Sunni domination in Iraq was seen by Iran as an opportunity to shift power to the Shia there and elsewhere.

Shia have always been dissenters in the Arab world and champions of martyrdom, while resisting the Sunni dominance.

In Iraq, there is interference by Al Qaeda, but the fundamental conflict is between Shia and Sunni which in fact results in most of the killing of Muslims. The Iranians are known to supply Iraqis with explosive devices and training, aimed at American forces. Iran would like to see the U.S. withdraw, thus showing weakness and allowing Iraq Shia cleric Al Sadr's Mahdi militia to control Iraq.

The slogan of the Tehran regime is "Death to Americans" and "the destruction of Israel". Its present leadership is intent on becoming a nuclear power and extending Shia influence.

Internally, Iran has serious economic problems and political unrest but the mullahs are still in control.

Nuclear Development

In 2003 the U.N. International Atomic Energy Agency discovered Iran had lied for years about its nuclear development in violation of its non-proliferation treaty. By 2006 Iran was completing the Bushehr nuclear power plant for peaceful energy, with Russia's help. It turns out the spent uranium fuel becomes plutonium which can be enriched with centrifuges to weapon grade, and Iran announced in 2007 it was completing the thousands of centrifuges in various locations to do so, claiming its right to have nuclear energy (in spite of its oil resources) is unrestricted. The U.N.'s weak sanction resolutions have been ignored.

It should be noted that the IAEA determined in 2003 that Iran had halted its program, but it is not known how near they are since then to having a nuclear bomb. Deadlines for cessation of development from the UN have not been met. U.S. negotiating through allies Germany, France and Britain has made no progress. Russia and China have opposed stronger UN sanctions.

Latest evaluations indicate Iran could have enriched uranium and the know how to build a bomb by 2010. Iran has tested Shahab missiles which have a range of 1500 miles.

Iran has also stated it will be willing to share its nuclear information with other Islamic nations, and they will attack U.S. (and Israeli) interests if we decide to bomb the Iranian nuclear facilities. The nuclear facilities are scattered and partially hidden.

Despite United Nations resolutions imposing sanctions on Iran for its non-compliance with IAEA International Atomic Energy Administration requirements, Iran publicly announced it is continuing enrichment of uranium. They claim it is not for weapon capability although it is not necessary for generating power for peaceful use. The enrichment process for uranium is the most critical part of nuclear weapons development along with missile capability which Iran is reportedly developing.

As for energy needs overall, Iran has one of the worlds' major supplies of oil and natural gas.

U.S. policy at present is to solicit the aid of countries in the region of Iran, to pressure the regime into halting its weapons development, which is its strategy for enhancing Iran's political influence.

NUCLEAR THREATS

United States Position

In order to end World War II which had been initiated by German and Japanese aggression, the U.S. demonstrated the power of atomic bombs in August 1945. The cities of Hiroshima and Nagasaki in Japan suffered over 115,000 deaths as a result, and Japan surrendered a week later. Continuing military destruction and casualties on both sides were thus avoided, and the message was clear to the whole world that nuclear bombs could destroy civilization. After the earlier defeat of Germany, the U.S. played a leading role in reconstruction there as well as in Japan.

Even in the prolonged cold war with Communist Russia, no nuclear weapons have been used in conflict since the ending of World War II. Nuclear weapons in the hands of peaceful powers are a strong deterrent, and defensive anti-missile systems are being developed.

Current Status

In the period from 1970 to 1990 the U.S. held as many as 27,000 nuclear weapons and the Soviet Union ultimately had 37,000. Non-proliferation treaties have reduced the number significantly.

The 1996 Comprehensive Test Ban Treaty has been signed by 177 nations, and ratified by 140 countries - but not yet the U.S. and China. It must have 44 countries who have some nuclear capability among the ratifiers, and only 34 so far have approved.

The Strategic Offensive Reductions Treaty of 2003 between the U.S. and Russia committed both to reducing nuclear warheads to 1700 to 2200 units each by 2012, and progress has been made.

Number of Nuclear Weapons by country in 2007:

United States	5200 plus 4800 inactive
Soviet/Russia	5700 plus 9300 inactive
China	400
France	350
United Kingdom	200
India	100 approx.
Pakistan	100 approx.
Isreal	100 estimated or less
North Korea	6 unconfirmed

Countries that were formerly part of the Soviet Union had on hand enriched uranium produced by Russia. There have been incidents in the past where small amounts of this material were offered for sale by smugglers who were caught. Since 2004 Russia has implemented a program which returned about 1,000 pounds of nuclear fuel to high security storage in Russia.

Other nations are discussed in separate sections.

North Korea

Background

North Korea is bound by China, Russia, South Korea and the Sea of Japan. It is relatively small in size, population and wealth. After World War II, a strict Communist regime has controlled the nation. Freedom and religion have been suppressed.

The Korean War (with the United States intervening in defense of South Korea) ended in a cease-fire after three years of conflict (in which China supported the North Korean military). A demilitarized zone was established between the two Koreas and China withdrew its military. The U.S. maintains a presence at the request of South Korea.

North Korea's economy is very poor and starving exists. In contrast, South Korea is a free and prospering democracy.

The North Korean government has devoted over a quarter of the country's gross domestic product to building a million-man army from its population of 23 million. Neighboring countries fear mass migration into their nations because of the North Koreans' poor living conditions.

Nuclear Development

In 1994, the Clinton administration negotiated with dictator Kim Jung Il to provide oil and non-plutonium reactors to North Korea in return for their giving up nuclear weapons development. In 2002 North Korea admitted they had continued their development program.

Earlier, North Korea had signed the international Non-Proliferation Treaty, only to withdraw from it later. The U.S. had removed its nuclear weapons from South Korea. North Korea since then has evaded UN inspections and violated more agreements with U.S. Republican administrations. Applying UN sanctions has been stalled by China, while China and others have provided food and fuel for the North Korean people.

In 2006 North Korea tested missiles in the Sea of Japan over the protests of China, South Korea and Japan. South Korea and Japan have upgraded their defense systems in response.

North Korea has plutonium material, claims to possess nuclear bombs, and reportedly tested an atomic explosive device as well as long range missiles. They have sold conventional military weapons in the Middle East and intelligence agencies advise they also have chemical weapons of mass destruction. We are concerned that they could sell weapons or knowhow to terrorists or rogue states.

North Korea has secretly aided Syria in building a nuclear facility, which Israel bombed in September 2007.

At our instigation, six party talks including North Korea's neighbors have been pursued in an effort to halt the nuclear weapons program again through diplomacy. They have begun disabling their plutonium reactor and have promised full disclosure in return for economic aid. But the newest agreement is still a work in progress.

North Korea thus far has been successful in negotiating for external aid and not living up to its commitments for disarmament.

China

Size

The People's Republic of China clearly is among the most important countries on our planet and a giant developing nation. Its population of 1 1/3 billion people represents 20 percent of the world's population (followed by 1 1/8 billion in India). The land area of 3.6 million square miles is a vast natural resource. Shanghai has a population of 15 million, but the capital city is Beijing.

History

China was ruled by emperor dynasties for thousands of years. Other nations had a presence in the country during the period before it consolidated into a republic in the early 1900's. From 1895 to 1945 China and Japan had conflicts over Japanese aggression.

After World War II the Communist Party took charge and a treaty with Russia was signed. During the United States and Korean War (which the U.S. entered to protect South Korea from the North) the Chinese army joined the fight in 1950 in behalf of North Korea, leading to a stalemate.

In 1971-72 the UN accepted China as a member, and the U.S. established diplomatic relations.

Culture

The official language is Mandarin. The prominent religions are Buddhism, Taoism, and Atheism. Literacy is 90 percent. GDP is relatively low for the size of the population, but is growing fast at ten percent per year. Millions still live in poverty.

There is a long established culture of respect, modesty, family orientation, pride, education, and industriousness, offset by governmental control and a lack of disclosure.

Change

China is in a transition from agrarian to an industrial nation, and from a socialist state toward a democracy. Because of its size and culture, the process of modernization has been slow. However, the growth rate in recent years has been impressive.

The structure of Communist party dominated government is responding to public pressure for more representation, human rights, and less nationalization of property. Relationships with Taiwan and Tibet are unsettled.

Through the UN where China is one of five members of the Security Council , China plays a role in the balance of power with the U.S. and the other nations. It is also a possessor of nuclear weapons which is a deterrent to aggressors.

International trade has been critical to China's economic progress. Exports are one trillion dollars annually and imports $800 billion. China's importation of oil has altered the world's supply and demand of that commodity.

U.S. diplomatic relations with China are still sensitive. We cannot interfere with their internal affairs nor change their culture, except through peaceful persuasion and diplomatic discourse. Sticky issues remain over pollution, human rights, trade imbalance, and military provocations.

OIL

Supply and Demand

Oil is plentiful although the supply will not last forever. The amount under the earth's surface will last for decades even at today's high usage rate. The modern world has a fully developed infrastructure to find it, produce and transport the fluid for energy uses. There is an inherent complication that most of the supply is in a few countries and most of the demand is in a different few countries.

OPEC the Organization of Petroleum Exporting countries is a cartel that is dependent on the revenue, but at the same time controls the flow of this commodity. Disruptions in the supply or anxiety about possible disruptions affect the price. Below ground reserves are estimated in the trillions of barrels. Inventories on hand vary but act as a buffer in case of disruptions.

Demand

The use of oil for heating, transportation, etc. is growing fast in China, India and the other developing nations. The U.S. is currently the largest user nation at about 25% of annual production. Oil accounts for two thirds of the world's energy consumption, followed by natural gas and coal.

Current major users:

(million barrels per day)

United States	21
Europe	16
China	9
Middle East	7
Asia Minor	6
Latin America	5
Japan	5
Russia	4
Africa	3
India	3

China's industrialization and population are projected to double and redouble its use of oil. India's ratio of vehicles per person using fuel is low but growing rapidly.

Supply

Some countries such as Russia, Canada, and Nigeria have increased production. Others including the U.S. and Venezuela have slowly declining production. The Middle East producers operate near capacity.

The U.S. imports unrefined oil from OPEC members and others. We currently produce 42% of our own crude oil needs.

Shares of the world crude oil production (%):

Saudi Arabia	14
Russia	12
United States	8
Mexico	5
Iran	5
Canada	4
Venezuela	4
Nigeria	3
Iraq	2
Other Middle East, etc.	43

Share of U.S. oil supply (%):

Canada	11
Mexico	11
Saudi Arabia	9
Venezuela	8
Nigeria	7
Iraq	4
Other Africa, etc.	8
United States	42

Our supply would be enhanced by more offshore drilling as in the Gulf of Mexico and elsewhere. The last coastal oil spill was in 1969, except for one later in Prudhoe Bay Alaska.

The ANWAR Alaska nature wildlife reserve proposal is to drill (with environmental safeguards) in two thousand acres of barren land contained in a **19 million** acre area populated by caribou.

The U.S. government holds about two months supply of import quantities in a strategic petroleum reserve for emergencies.

Risks

The twelve OPEC countries are Angola, Ecuador, Indonesia, Iran, Iraq, Kuwait, Libya, Nigeria, Qatar, Saudi Arabia, United Arab Emirates, and Venezuela. They are all very dependent on export oil revenues to sustain their economies. The global market can be manipulated by OPEC decisions to raise or lower production and affect prices.

Fully 90 percent of the world's proven crude oil reserves are owned by a country or are government controlled.

Transportation of oil is particularly vulnerable for ships in the straits of the Middle East. Pipelines elsewhere are also vulnerable to damage. Terrorist attacks for political reasons are the newest threat to oil production and refining facilities.

On shore and off shore production are frequently halted in one area or another by natural disasters such as hurricanes, or by fiery accidents.

There are so few oil producing countries that disruption of production for whatever reason has an impact on the world balance of supply and demand.

Prices

The international market does <u>not</u> set the prices for crude oil based only upon supply and demand. In the commodity exchanges there is trader activity of bid and asked prices, but the seller has a bargaining advantage because the need is greater for the buyer of the commodity. There is little competition among the sellers except for differences in location and heavy versus light crude oil which is easier to refine.

Prices fluctuate dramatically based on **speculation** about future supply and demand, natural disasters, geopolitical risks and the popularity of commodities over other investments. Furthermore the betting on futures in the commodity exchange allows low margin deposits in order to enter into a contract, increasing speculation on higher prices.

Price is also affected by the exchange value of the dollar, and this carries over to international oil prices which are usually in dollars.

Since 2001 the price of crude has risen from $30 per barrel to more than **$130**, in a period of low inflation. At current U.S. usage levels, each $10 per barrel cost change amounts to $73 billion per year. Prices have increased most recently at an irrational rate. The average price in 2005 was $50 per barrel, in 2006 $60 to $70, in 2007 $70 to $90.

While the U.S. uses mostly gasoline for vehicles, much of the world uses diesel fuel in cars as well as trucks. The taxes on diesel in Europe make it and gasoline higher priced than in the U.S.

Gasoline

The U.S. consumes over nine million barrels or 500 million gallons per day. Gasoline is the most volatile element in the CPI consumer price index.

Retail gasoline price trends:

2003	up 17 %
2004	up 18 %
2005	up 20 %
2006	up 12 %
2007	up 30 %
2008	up 40 % to date at $4.00 per gallon

The cost breakdown of gasoline at $2.50 per gallon retail:

Crude oil content	56 %
Refining cost and profits	18 %
Distribution and marketing expense and profit	5 %
State and Federal taxes	21 %

In the 1970's recessionary period, Republican and Democratic administrations tried price controls on petroleum. The result was reduced investment in drilling and refining, plus no actual reduction in prices. In the 1980's a windfall profit tax on the oil companies caused a decline in domestic production and an increase in imports. The major U.S. oil companies pay taxes in an amount approximately equal to their net profit.

America only has refining capacity for 85% of the volume needed, because of lack of investment incentive in the past and restrictive environmental regulations. No new refinery has been built in the U.S. in decades and expansion of existing facilities has been limited. Thus, we import 15% of our gasoline.

Alternative Fuels

The automotive industry is busy developing "hybrid" electric, compressed gas and other vehicle power systems for consumers to consider. We must recognize that alternative energy systems for engines and other applications would already be used more extensively if they were economical and we had in place the necessary supporting infrastructure.

Many power plants for generating electricity use coal which is plentiful but a challenge to reduce pollution, water power is used where it is suitable, and natural gas is widely used in stationary applications. We have 100 nuclear power plants in operation in America. Wind and solar power use are on the increase.

For vehicles, hydrogen fuel cells are in the experimental stage. Waste oils are being reprocessed on a limited scale. Biodiesel fuel from plant and animal oils may be comparable to diesel oil in many respects, but sufficient agriculture and refining process capabilities are yet to be put in place. Grasses require tremendous quantities to produce ethanol.

Ethanol

Congress has passed legislation mandating the increased use of ethanol in America's 150 million autos and light trucks. Ten to fifteen percent ethanol is prevalent in gasoline now but engines need some modification for **E85** which is 85% ethanol fuel.

Ethanol yields lower miles per gallon than gasoline, and the E85 mix requires major capital investment not only in refineries but in transportation and storage equipment because of corrosion, etc.

Ethanol production uses lots of water, requires crop land otherwise used to produce food, and takes considerable energy to grow and process it. However, pollution levels are reduced as is dependence on fossil fuel.

Ethanol is produced in the U.S. from corn and in Brazil from sugar cane and sugar beets. The U.S. government is subsidizing the production of ethanol with 50 cents per gallon incentive, and private capital is being invested.

A somewhat unforeseen by-product of the increased demand for corn is higher prices for many foods affected by the increased allocation to fuel use, which extends beyond corn to other grains, livestock feed, the price of farmland, etc. Corn was $2.00 per bushel in 2006 and is over $6.00 in 2008. This year 30% of the domestic corn crop will be diverted to the production of ethanol.

PAST CRISES

With the ubiquitous around the clock television news coverage today you might think there is a major crisis every day. However, there is a difference of great magnitude in the latest news flash about some on the spot news event that affects few people, compared to real and important serious crises that occur over time and have historic importance. Typhoons and earthquakes do kill thousands in some areas of the world.

Even natural disasters in our own country such as coastal hurricanes and tornadoes damage sizable amounts of property as well as cause some deaths and injuries. But these and most economic downturns, like the current mortgage credit problem, may not be classified as major crises like wars. Starvation and diseases in undeveloped places like Africa are a real major problem and humanitarian crises, but not easily solved by external efforts.

The Great Depression

One exception (other than American involvement in wars) was the worst economic depression in U.S. history in the 1930's. The collapse of banks and record unemployment affected millions for several years. The unemployment level reached twenty percent. The government funded massive public works projects nationwide.

Cold War

The prolonged threat of nuclear war between the Soviet Union and the U.S. after World War II fortunately did not produce a real shooting conflict, but does qualify as a major crisis because if not settled would have been the greatest tragedy ever.

9/11/2001

The attack by radical Islamists on the U.S. World Trade Center buildings in New York City with high-jacked jet airliners was historic in that it was the first attack on American soil since the Revolution, and killed 3,000 citizens instantly. It demonstrated terrorism and anti-Americanism by Al Qaeda on a new scale.

Wars

Wars are fought over power, greed, hatred, land, religion, freedom, persecution, insults or other grievances.

The **Civil War** (1861-1865) between the north and south over states' rights, slavery, and secession ended in a victory for the union but at incredible cost. The Union forces suffered 360,000 deaths from battle and other causes, the Confederates 134,000 deaths; plus several hundred thousand wounded on both sides. One thing remembered from the war is Lincoln's eloquent Gettysburg address. The union of the new nation was preserved and the practice of slavery ended with the emancipation proclamation.

World War I (1914-1918) was brought on by Germany's attempt to take over Europe. America came to the aid of allies. In winning, we suffered 117,000 deaths and 204,000 wounded. New tools of war such as aircraft were used.

World War II was the most expansive and destructive in world history. In 1939 Germany again invaded other European countries with Hitler's intent to conquer the continent, if not the world. His regime also committed genocide against six million Jews. Most of Europe became a battleground.

The U.S. responded when the Japanese, with empirical ambitions in the Pacific, joined Germany and attacked the U.S. at Pearl Harbor, Hawaii on December 7, 1941. The U.S., Russia, Britain and other allies defeated Germany in 1944 and with the atomic bombs defeated Japan in 1945. Casualty totals were in the millions.

America's conversion of industry to production of military equipment was remarkable. The Marshall Plan for recovery in Europe after the war was also very successful.

The United Nations was established in 1945 to provide a forum for all countries to communicate and to seek worldwide peace. NATO also was formed by the U.S. and European allies, now expanded to include part of eastern Europe.

Communism grew in China and the Soviet Union. Its spread in Asia was halted by U.S. intervention. The U.S. blockaded Russian missile installation in Cuba. The cold war with Russia ended with the opening of East Berlin.

The **Korean War** started with the U.S. defending South Korea after an attack by the north. The Chinese military aided the north. An armistice in 1953 set up a demilitarized zone and the two Koreas agreed to work toward reunification, but the north regimes chose isolation. South Korea has since flourished. U.S. deaths totaled 36,000.

The **Vietman War** began with U.S. defense of South Vietnam after the communist north invasion in 1965. Peace talks began in 1969. The war was very unpopular in America. Battle resumed in 1971, but U.S. troops withdrew from Saigon in 1972, having lost 58,000 lives. Vietnam eventually became more democratic and U.S. relations improved by the 1990's.

AMERICA COMPARED

Principles

The U.S. form of democracy is based upon individual freedoms, government that protects the people, free markets and capitalism, majority rule, morals and work ethic. We have our share of social problems, but the strengths to cope with them and an enviable standard of living.

Unlike the underdeveloped nations, America is prosperous and provides the bulk of our population with a comfortable lifestyle, setting an example for others. We also give twice as much as most countries to others.

G-8 Group of Eight

Among the leading nations of the world, the U.S. sets the standard for production of food, scientific research, development of new technologies, communication systems, equitable treatment of people and religious tolerance.

A tangible measure of prosperity and standard of living is GDP per capita. That is the national income from a year's production of goods and services in dollar value per person.

2006 GDP Per Capita ($ billion)

United States	44
Canada	36
Japan	33
United Kingdom	32
Germany	32
France	31
Italy	30
Russia	12

Russia was recently added to the original G-7 but is not a full member. China, India, and Brazil are being proposed as additional members of this group of industrialized nations.

COMPARISON OF NATIONS

	Type of Government	Population (millions)	Area (thousand square miles)	GDP (billion dollars)	Active Military (thousands)
Afghanistan	Islamic Republic	32	250	22	50
Brazil	Federal Republic	190	3286	1700	288
China	Communist State	1322	3705	10,200	2,255
France	Republic	63	211	1,900	255
Germany	Federal Republic	82	138	2,600	246
India	Federal Republic	1130	1269	4,200	1,316
Indonesia	Republic	234	741	948	302
Iran	Islamic Republic	65	636	599	545
Iraq	Constitutional Democracy	28	169	51	227
Israel	Republic	6	8	170	168
Italy	Republic	58	116	1,800	191
Japan	Parliamentary Democracy	127	146	4,200	240
Mexico	Federal Republic	109	762	1,100	238

COMPARISON OF NATIONS

	Type of Government	Population (millions)	Area (thousand square miles)	GDP (billion dollars)	Active Military (thousands)
North Korea	Communist Dictatorship	23	47	40	1,106
Pakistan	Military Republic	165	310	438	619
Russia	Federal Republic	141	593	1,700	1,027
Saudi Arabia	Monarchy	28	757	366	225
South Korea	Republic	49	38	1,200	687
Spain	Constitutional Monarchy	40	195	1,100	147
Syria	Military Republic	19	78	72	308
Taiwan	Democracy	23	14	681	290
Turkey	Republic	71	301	636	515
United Kingdom	Constitutional Monarchy	61	95	1,900	191
United States	Federal Democratic Republic	301	3719	13,100	1,507

The Role of Government

America was founded by immigrants from Europe seeking a more free and better life. As the new country's organization evolved it became a representative democracy and federation of states. Three branches of government were formed to provide a balance of power. The Constitution establishes individual rights and places limitations on the role of government.

Bill of Rights

The first Amendment guarantees freedom of religion, speech, the press, right of assembly, and to petition for grievances. Other amendments express a right to bear arms, due process of law, trial by jury, no unreasonable search or seizure, no excess fines or cruel punishment.

Powers not assigned to the federal government are delegated to the states.

Amendment XIII abolished slavery in 1865. Other succeeding amendments cover civil rights, elections, and commerce.

Legislation

Congress has the power to impose taxes, spend money, regulate commerce, declare war, coin money, and enact other national laws not reserved for the states. The House of Representatives and Senate are elected by the people.

Executive Power

The president is Commander in chief of the military. He appoints senior officials and makes treaties with approval of the Senate. The President administers the functions of government through departments such as Defense, State, Commerce, Justice etc.

Judicial

The U.S. Supreme Court decides cases involving the Constitution, treaties, interstate legal issues, and federal court appeals. Congress establishes lower federal courts. With Senate approval the President appoints federal judges for life.

Military

Congress establishes and funds a military force. The President appoints senior officers. Congress has the power to declare war. The Commander in Chief directs military actively in war and peace, through a chain of command. If a draft for military service is needed, Congress must enact legislation. The military is subordinate to elected officials who determine national policy.

It should be noted that the President receives praise and criticism for national successes and for problems. Currently this includes public concern about war and the economy. Congress is sometimes criticized for partisan politics and inaction or for excessive taxation and spending.

Size of Government

In 2007 there were **2.7** million civilian federal government employees and **1.4** million military personnel on active duty. There are countless departments, bureaus, agencies, offices, commissions and administrations – not counting numerous contract agents and services.

Political Parties

Ours is essentially a two party system although lesser independent parties may enter election contests. The Democratic party advocates an assertive role for government (the "liberal" view) particularly to aid people in need, the Republican ("conservative") party favors a limited role for government with free markets, low taxes and smaller government. The American system is not perfect but the results have been outstanding.

Lobbying

The citizenry can petition government as well as vote for representation in periodic elections. On an ongoing basis, organized solicitation to Congress and the administration is performed by lobbyists. Some cases of illegal influence have occurred, but legitimate lobbying is conducted by groups such as the American Association of Retired Persons, the National Education Association, Civil Rights organizations and many other worthy causes. Congressional representatives do insert "earmark" funding for their constituencies into legislative bills.

CONCLUSION

America is "alive and well", free and prosperous.

The economy and employment do go through cycles of growth and slowdown with occasional anxious moments caused by excesses. These moderate over time as corrective action such as taxes and interest rates cuts are applied. Jobs are created essentially by private enterprise.

It is true that our federal and local governments tax personal and corporate incomes progressively to provide funding for the huge expenditures approved by the administrations and legislatures. All too often these turn out to be less effective than expected or result in unintended consequences. Our healthcare system has deficiencies but it still is the best in the world, and social security is widespread and long established.

There is a strong human tendency to try to help others, equalize the distribution of wealth, and promote what we think is best for the world. However, the role of government has to be limited to allow for individual choice, and funding is not infinite.

The balance of power designed by this nation's founders restrains both how much the President can actually control and what Congress can do. The government works best when the electorate puts capable leaders in key positions and they work together, which is not always the case. The current level of dissatisfaction by a majority of our citizenry may be attributable not only to questionable policy decisions but also a reflection on poor leadership and conflicting objectives. In deliberations of the Senate a minority of 40% can block a vote by "fili-buster", in effect requiring a majority of 60% instead of a simple majority.

International issues have to be resolved through joint effort with other nations. The U.S. cannot impose its ways on other sovereign countries, but we are in a position to lead and have strong implied power to influence.

In today's global interdependence we certainly must not engage in trade wars or practice self isolation through protectionism.

We are the largest users of oil but the supply is mostly from other countries. Not only can we bargain over the supply, but we can independently convert a significant portion of our usage to alternative fuels. The answer to the cost and potential scarcity of this commodity is not to argue further over which alternative is best, because none of them is sufficient on its own. The solution is to proceed with implementing all of the proposed alternative energy developments, along with increased domestic oil drilling and refining, at a faster pace. Some of these will succeed and some may not but "nothing ventured nothing gained". More mass transit will save fuel, but requires a change in our habits and substantial capital investment.

Nuclear threats of Iran, North Korea, and others should be reduced through existing UN/IAEA procedures, plus negotiation by the U.S. and its partners with those seeking to acquire nuclear weapons. Our deterrent of the U.S. retaining military nuclear capabilities is a back up necessity. We must be watchful that another Hitler or fanatic does not lead a country toward nuclear war.

The war in Iraq has gone on too long, and we must press harder for the Iraqis to take control. Once the conflict has subsided, critics will re-evaluate the gains and the costs so we can learn from the experience. Iraq and the wealthy neighboring Arab countries should pay more toward reconstruction.

Al Qaeda is expected to reappear elsewhere, until they are defeated decisively.

Palestinians need to accept a land for peace deal with Israel. It is the way they can have their own country.

Islam and the traditional Muslim faith are not a problem for the western world, except for the radical elements who use religion as a justification for mass murders of innocent people to achieve power. These extremists and supporters of terrorism must be confronted by all the peaceful Arab and Muslim countries, whether the governments are Islamic or secular.

The centuries old issue between Sunni and Shia Muslims is not likely to be resolved as long as Iran is dominated by extremist clergy and radical politicians, but changes in regime should originate internally.

In this American election year, politicians and the media exaggerate negative news and opinions. Candidates claim to have wonderful solutions to every issue. Unfortunately, the government cannot cure all problems, especially those brought on by lack of individual responsibility and those which are non-public matters.

There are legitimate points of disagreement over taxation to provide more benefits, war on terror balanced with defense of liberties, diplomatic strategies, terrorists, isolationism versus globalization and free trade, immigration, energy and the environment.

There is no easy and perfect solution to these complex problems, but partial and acceptable solutions are achievable. The answers will come from evaluation of facts, rational and civil debate, agreement on principles, balancing opposing points of view with compromise, prudent judgment, and restrained exercise of power.

These are challenging times but our system of individual freedom, representative democracy, capitalism, and desire for peace will prevail as it has throughout most of our history.

———— reach your own conclusions.

Tables and Illustrations

Sources:

Employment Data	U.S. Department of Labor
Stock Market Chart	Wall Street Journal data
Federal Budget – table and graph	Office of Management and Budget
Tax Shares	Internal Revenue Service
Middle East Map	National Geographic
Nuclear Weapons Count	Various sources
Oil Users and Producers	Energy Information Administration
Gasoline Prices	Energy Information Administration
Leading Countries GDP	World Trade Organization

Comparison of Nations data partially extracted from the World Almanac and Book of Facts.

Glossary

AMT	Alternative Minimum Tax
Al Qaeda	International Islamic Terrorist Organization
Baath Party	Iraq Sunni political party
CIA	Central Intelligence Agency
CPI	Consumer Price Index
Crude Oil	Heavy or light, before refining
Economic Recession	Two quarters or more negative GDP
E85	85 percent Ethanol fuel
Fatah	Palestinian political faction
FISA	Foreign Intelligence Surveillance Act
FRB	Federal Reserve Board
GDP	Gross Domestic Product
Geneva Convention	International pact on conduct of War
G-8	Group of Eight industrialized countries
Hamas	Palestinian political faction
Hezbollah	Lebanese militants
IAEA	UN International Atomic Energy Agency
Jihad	Muslim religious war declaration
NAFTA	North American Free Trade Association

NATO	North Atlantic Treaty Organization
NIE	National Intelligence Estimates
NSA	National Security Agency
Occupied Territories	Gaza Strip and West Bank in Israel
OMB	Office of Management and Budget
OPEC	Organization of Petroleum Exporting Countries
Radical Islam	Seeking theocratic government and dominance of religion through violence
Secular	Government authority separated from religion
Shia, Shiite	Minority Muslim sect
Sunni	Majority Muslim sect
Terrorism	Intimidation by physical violence and fear
Wahabbi	Saudi Arab fundamentalist Muslims
WMD	Weapons of Mass Destruction

Index

93, 110
Senate Intelligence Committee
    67
Share of Taxes Paid 23
Size of Government 113
Social Security 16, 17, 21, 27,
    28, 29
Social Security Deficit 16, 17,
    21, 27, 28, 29, 115
Stock Market 7, 8, 24, 123
Sunni and Shia 60, 118
Syria 41, 60, 61, 64, 84, 110

T

Taliban 51, 63
Tax Cuts 24, 26
Tax Rates 9, 21
Tax Revenue Sources 24, 29
Tax System Problems 22
Terrorism 47, 48, 51, 53, 54,
    55, 69, 72, 102, 118, 126
Trade (International) 11, 13,
    14, 49, 50, 87, 102, 116,
    118, 123, 125

U

U.S. Troop Withdrawal 59, 71,
    105
Unemployment 1, 4, 8, 9, 13,
    29, 70, 102
Uninsured (Healthcare) 33
UN United Nations 19, 63, 74,
    75, 78, 104

V

Vietnam War 60, 105

W

WMD Weapons of Mass De-
    struction 60, 66, 126
World Religious Populations
    45, 46, 48, 55, 65, 72,
    108, 125

World War I 103
World War II 27, 41, 42, 60,
    79, 82, 85, 102, 103

Z

Zawahiri 51, 53

www.ingramcontent.com/pod-product-compliance
Lightning Source LLC
Chambersburg PA
CBHW020240290526
45784CB00003B/1051